PEACE OUT

CALM DOWN
WORKBOOK FOR KIDS

CHANEL TSANG
CREATOR OF *PEACE OUT PODCAST*

ILLUSTRATIONS BY CORY REID

Dedication

This book is dedicated to my daughters and the first *Peace Out* listeners, Katelyn and Erin, and to my husband, Caleb, whose love and support allow me to pursue my dreams. ILYWSYIMH.

Introduction for Grown-Ups

So often, children are asked to "calm down," but what does calm look like? What does it feel like?

Created in 2017, *Peace Out Podcast* was one of the first children's podcasts focused on mindfulness and social-emotional learning. The format is a unique blend of fun science facts and mindfulness breathing exercises—they're not quite stories and not a straight meditation, but something about it just works! Like the podcast, this book focuses on demonstrating and modeling empathy and inclusion, with the hope that if we can reach a child when they are 6, then perhaps they'll be comfortable advocating for themselves and others at 16 (or earlier!).

The best way to use this book? Read it together and do the yoga and mindfulness activities as a team! Let your child lead the way, and remember, the best time to stop any activity with children is when they're still having fun. It's OK if they only want to do the yoga movement or only read the story one night. Let the book work for your child!

Peace out and peace within,

—CHANEL

Introduction Just for Kids

Welcome to the Calm Down Workbook for Kids!
Before you start exploring these relaxing stories
about whale sharks, constellations and geodes,
I'll let you in on a secret...the title of the book says
"workbook," but there's actually no work for you
to do! Here's what it's really about:

• **Fun facts** about space, animals, and other amazing
things on earth (did you know that capybaras are
related to guinea pigs?)

• **Relaxing** (and sometimes challenging) yoga moves
that are good for your brain and body

• **Mindfulness games and activities** that you can do
anytime on your own or with your family

When we said this was a workbook, we meant that
this book will be working for you! That's right,
YOU'RE THE BOSS here, you can pick which story to
start with or read them in order. You can choose to
just do a mindfulness game today and save the story
for tomorrow. You can read it on your own, or have
your grown up read it.

OK, I think that's it! Are you ready? Let's begin...

All About the Calm Down Countdown

On *Peace Out Podcast*, we do the Calm Down Countdown before we dive into a mindfulness story. What's the Countdown? It's our chance to press pause and just breathe. By the time you get from 10 to 1, you'll feel calmer and more relaxed.

In this book, you can do the Calm Down Countdown before each story. All you have to do is trace the number path and breathe. That's it!

Try it on the opposite page! Trace the path with your finger slowly (imagine you are visiting each little dot along the way).

Start to breathe in on the purple numbers.
Start to breathe out on the green numbers.

Breathe in... 10   8   6   4   2

Breathe out...   9   7   5   3   1

Try it again, but this time, go slower so your in and out breaths are longer. Take your time. Enjoy your breathing.

This book is packed with many mindfulness moments. Practicing mindfulness meditation means taking your time to pay attention. This could be paying attention to your thoughts, the sights and sounds around you, or anything that you notice happening right now in the present moment. It's relaxing and can help us calm down.

Mindfulness can also help you focus, feel less stressed and become more caring toward yourself and others—which is a very good thing!

Try it right now: How many things can you notice?

All done? Let's get started!

A Trip to the Moon

Let's pretend we're astronauts! We're sitting in our spaceship, waiting for launch. What color is your spaceship?

Are you ready to go? It's time to turn on our imaginations. You can close your eyes now if you'd like (unless you're reading, of course).

Let's take a deep breath in...and let it out. Keep focusing on your breathing as we count down slooowly...to lift off!

Breathe in...   10   8   6   4   2
                9   7   5   3   1

We made it! We're on the moon!

Now we're looking through the round spaceship window, out into space! You can see the gray surface of the moon below and the dark, dark expanse of space above. Picture yourself taking a BIG step outside.

The moon's gravity is much weaker than the gravity on Earth. Gravity is the force that pulls us and everything else toward the earth's core. If there were no gravity, nothing would keep us down and we'd float up up up! Since the moon's gravity is weaker, the pull-down is not as powerful, so objects on the moon float a little before coming back down. Take a moment now to imagine how much lighter you'd feel on the moon.

The moon goes through many phases and looks different each night.

This is a crescent moon. On the next page, we are going to do a crescent moon yoga pose!

11

Yoga Time

Let's make a crescent moon shape.

1 Raise your hands above your head, palms touching.

2 Let the tips of your fingers be the leaders and follow them as they *slowly* reach over to one side. There's our crescent moon!

3 Now let's come back to the center.

4 We're going to make a crescent moon on the other side. Slowly lean the other way. And come back to the center.

5 We're going to do this a few more times, but this time, we'll match our moves to our breathing.

6 When you lean to one side, breathe out. When you come back to the center, breathe in.

Well done! Repeat as many times as you'd like.

Mindful Moment

The moon has no atmosphere and no wind. That's why there are still boot prints on the moon from astronauts who walked there decades ago! The boot prints will be there for a long, long time.

If you wrote your name on the moon's surface, it would be there for your entire life! It would be **YOUR** special spot. Trace or write your name on the moon here.

Now trace your name on your hand. You can close your eyes and picture yourself on the quiet, peaceful moon. Breathe in and out. Whenever you need a break, you can revisit your special spot on the moon and take some deep breaths.

And when you're ready, come back down to Earth, recharged and refreshed!

Whale Sharks

We're going on an ocean adventure!
Let's use our imaginations and pretend
we're in our very own submarine.

Sit up tall and proud in your captain's chair.
Close your eyes if you'd like. Relax...and breathe.

Breathe in... 10   8   6   4   2

Breathe out...   9   7   5   3   1

Whale sharks live in tropical oceans and are the
largest fish in the sea. They can grow to become
the length of a school bus! They are dark gray with
light spots all over their back and have a white
belly and a flat snout. Whale sharks are also an
endangered species.

Whale sharks don't use their teeth
much when eating. Instead,
they filter feed. What's filter
feeding? Well, whale sharks
have what are called filter
pads in front of their throats
that act like a strainer.

Fun Fact

Scientists believe that
the pattern of spots
on each whale shark's
back may be one-of-
a-kind, just like our
fingerprints!

They suck in the water around them, and any nearby shrimp, small fish or plankton (their favorite!) get caught in the filter pads. The seawater then passes through large gills that also work like backup strainers, letting out the water and catching any food all in one go.

Design Your Own Whale Shark

Draw the pattern here using lines, circles and dots. Your pattern will be unique—just like you!

Yoga Time

1 Lie down on your belly with your chin resting on the ground. Your arms are by your sides and your legs are straight out behind you.

2 Take a deep breath in and lift everything off the ground: your head, shoulders, arms and legs. Look down at the floor, just in front of you. Breathe out and relax back down onto the floor, looking to one side.

3 Try that again, and when you come back down, look to the other side.

You did it! Repeat as many times as you'd like.

Mindful Moment

Your mind is a thought machine, automatically making many thoughts non-stop. That's a good thing: Our brains are working!

Helpful thoughts give us information about the world and about ourselves. We can learn from them. These thoughts can also just make us feel good, like remembering a funny joke. (Here's one: Why couldn't the pony sing? Because she was a little horse!)

Unhelpful thoughts can be thoughts that make us feel scared, worried or anxious. Everyone has unhelpful thoughts sometimes and usually they go away or turn into helpful thoughts. (If you feel that your unhelpful thoughts are not going away*, talk about it with a grown-up you trust.)

Pretend your thoughts are bubbles. For the next few seconds, try to notice your thought bubbles as they come up. You don't have to figure out whether they're helpful or unhelpful, just notice them and then watch the bubbles float away. Try it now.

How was that? Did you notice many thoughts? How do you feel right now?

Remember, just as every bubble eventually pops, all thoughts (even the negative ones) will eventually float away.

Want to learn how you can deal with unhelpful thoughts? Go to pg. 40.

*This is different than when we have thoughts that make us a little worried or a little scared, because those feelings can help us. For example, if you feel a *little* worried about a test, that can become helpful because it makes you study more to get ready or realize you need extra help. If you are *very* worried about something (or many things) all the time, you can talk about it with a grown-up you trust.

Green-Eyed Monsters:
Jealousy and Envy

These emotions can be difficult to deal with—they bring out negativity and make us feel bad about ourselves. But everyone feels jealous or envious sometimes; that's normal. What matters is how you deal with how you feel.

Jealousy is feeling like we might lose something we already have. Someone might feel jealous if their best friend starts playing with the new kid in school because they think they might lose their friendship.

Envy is wanting something that someone else has. Someone might feel envious of someone who has a newer bike.

Jealousy and envy are like BFFs—they're often found together.

These two emotions affect everyone differently. For example, we might not feel happy for others when they do well or when good things happen to them.

One excellent way to help get over feeling jealous or envious is to focus on gratitude, which means being thankful for what you already have. Thinking of all the different things that are good in our lives fills our minds up with positive thoughts, which pushes out the negative ones! Write or draw what (or who) you're thankful for below and see which people, places or things come to mind.

Today, I am grateful for...

Yoga Time

1 Sit in a comfortable position. With your hands on your knees, start to squeeze them into fists. Squeeze harder now, feeling your arms and hands getting tenser and tighter. Let's pretend these are jealous feelings.

2 Now, release your fists. Let your hands and arms relax and feel them gently melt. The tension and tightness are leaving.

3 Shake out your arms and relax.

Mindful Moment

Another way to handle envy is to remember the times you did well at something. You can think about these memories and feel proud of yourself and what you accomplished. It can also help to think about the things you like about yourself. What is something

you're good at?
Maybe you're always
kind to animals or
are good at drawing
or karate.

Write or draw
three things about
yourself that you like
or feel proud of.
Come back and add
more any time you like!

Did You Know?

Ancient Greeks believed
jealousy was caused by too much
bile in our bodies (a liquid made by
our livers to help us digest food).
They thought it made those people's
faces look green! Later,
William Shakespeare coined the
phrase "green-eyed monster"
in his play *Othello*.

What are you proud of?

Pomelo

What's your favorite type of fruit?

Aren't we lucky to live in a world where there are so many different types of fruit, all with unique flavors and ways to enjoy them?

Speaking of things we enjoy, let's start with the Calm Down Countdown. When you do it this time, focus on enjoying your breathing!

Trace the path with your finger, breathing in with the purple numbers and out with the green numbers.

Breathe in... 10   8   6   4   2

Breathe out...   9   7   5   3   1

Have you ever eaten a pomelo? It's a relative of the grapefruit and comes from Southeast Asia, including Indonesia (in-doh-NEE-zha) and Malaysia (mah-LAY-zha). It tastes like a sweet grapefruit! Pomelos can be round or pear-shaped and come in three varieties: white, red and pink. They contain a lot of vitamin C.

These fruits look a lot like grapefruits but have a thicker green or yellow peel. The outside part of the

POMELO

LEMON

LIME

ORANGE

The pomelo's scientific name is *Citrus maxima*, which means "the biggest citrus."

peel (called the rind) can be smooth or a little bumpy. When ripe, pomelos can weigh about 2 to 4 pounds (1 to 2 kilograms), big enough that you need both hands to hold one!

Fruits are versatile, which means they can be used in many different ways. You can cook them, add them to salads or eat them on their own! In the Philippines, people combine pomelo and pineapple juice to make a refreshing drink. Many people in Sri Lanka like to eat pomelo as dessert, sprinkling it with sugar. You can even make candied pomelo peel by boiling pieces of the peel in water and then letting it soak up sugar syrup! Yum!

Yoga Time

❶ The Legs-up-the-Wall Pose is great for calming down. It's a perfect exercise to do before bedtime (or anytime you want to relax!).

❷ For this yoga pose, you will need a wall with enough space in front of it for you to lie down. Check with a grown-up if you aren't sure.

❸ Lie down in front of an empty wall with your knees bent and the tips of your toes touching the wall.

❹ Walk your feet up the wall, moving your bottom closer too until your legs can relax against the wall (you should look like an "L" shape!)

❺ Put your arms by your sides, palms up.

❻ Rest and relax like this as long as you like.

❼ When you're ready to come out of this pose, bend your knees and roll to one side.

Mindful Moment

EATING WITH OUR SENSES

What You Need
- Your favorite fruit
- Knife
- Cutting board (optional)

Ask a grown-up to help you with this activity!

SEE Take a moment to look at your fruit. Pretend to describe it to an alien who's never seen one before.

TOUCH What does it feel like? Is it smooth, bumpy or rough? Heavy or light?

SMELL Give it a sniff. Is there a strong smell? Does the scent remind you of anything?

HEAR If you and your grown-up need to peel or cut the fruit, pay attention to the sounds as you do.

TASTE Take a small bite. Hold it in your mouth for a few seconds. Focus on the taste and texture (soft, hard, smooth, rough)...then finish your delicious snack!

Water Cycle
(Relaxation Read Aloud)

Before we splash into the water cycle, let's press pause and do the Calm Down Countdown. Take a moment to notice how you're feeling right now. Are you feeling happy, upset, sad, indifferent? However you feel, it's OK. You can put it to the side for now as you just focus on your breathing...

Trace the path with your finger, breathing in with the purple numbers and out with the green numbers.

Breathe in...   10   8   6   4   2

Breathe out...   9   7   5   3   1

How do you feel now? Hopefully, a little bit calmer. Hold on to that feeling.

When rain falls to the earth, we're seeing part of the wonderful water cycle! Why is it wonderful? The water cycle is how water moves through the air and the earth to make life possible for all living things.

You've seen it in action, too! After the rain falls to the earth, the raindrops help water the plants and trees. They might join rivers, lakes or oceans or form puddles. We all need water to live, so the water cycle is important.

During the water cycle, water goes through all three of its states of matter:

When it's raining and when the water is moving through the oceans, it's **liquid**.

When it's snowing or hailing, it's **solid**.

When it is heated up and becomes water vapor, it's **gas**.

Next time it's raining, spend some time listening to the rain pitter patter outside. You can close your eyes and enjoy the beautiful sounds of nature and maybe say thank you to the rain (and water cycle) for giving us the gift of life!

On the next page, let's pretend to be a raindrop riding through the water cycle.

Raindrop Ride

Let's pretend to be a little drop of water going through the water cycle!

Sit however you feel comfortable. Close your eyes if you'd like. Think about your breathing feels and sounds as you breathe in and out three times on your own.

Imagine you're a tiny drop of water. Liquid. In the condensation part of the water cycle, you're part of a cloud, floating around with other water drops in the air. Wave your body from left to right...left to right...left to right. Make your movements shorter as more and more water droplets come closer together.

The cloud is too heavy now, and you start to fall. This is the precipitation part of the water cycle. (Lie down and close your eyes if you like).
Now you're a raindrop and you're getting closer to the earth. Feel the wind rushing past your ears.

Splash! Some of your raindrop friends land on soil and become groundwater to help feed the plants and animals.

Splash! Other raindrops fall into the ocean.

Splash! You've just landed nicely into a river. The water is cool, and now you're going for a ride down the river. Pretend you're on a slide as you glide down a waterfall (whee!) and into a beautiful pool. Splash!

The sun is shining down on you and you're getting warmer and warmer. Suddenly, you're not liquid anymore—the heat changed you into a gas! You're in the evaporation stage now, floating back up in the air. The earth looks smaller and smaller as you rise into the bright blue sky.

As the chilly air cools you down, a lot of the water droplets huddle together and form a cloud. We're back in the condensation part of the water cycle. Soon we'll turn back into liquid rain and fall to earth to begin the cycle again. What a ride!

Put one hand on your heart and one hand on your belly. Notice how your body moves as you're breathing. Breathe and relax. You can relive this journey whenever you like.

Yoga Time

Water can fit into
any container, no matter the
size or shape. See if
you can position your body
so you would fit into any
(or all!) of these shapes:
triangle, circle, square,
star, heart, cross or L.

Mindful Moment

Let's create a rainstick!

Check with your grown-up before starting
this activity.

What You Need
- Pencil or pen
- Paper towel tube
- Colorful paper/
  washi tape
- Scissors
- Tape or glue
- Tinfoil
- Rice or beans
- Rubber bands
  (optional)

1 With a pencil or pen, trace two circles using the
end of your paper towel tube on paper, leaving at

least 2 inches of extra space around the circles. Cut out the circles.

❷ Decorate your tube using paper strips cut out from the construction paper and/or washi tape.

❸ Twist a sheet of tin foil into a coil that is as long as the tube. Put it into the tube.

❹ Add a spoonful of rice or beans.

❺ Close off the ends with your paper circles. Secure with rubber bands or tape.

❻ Slowly tilt the rainstick back and forth and see if you can make it sound like it's raining! Try closing your eyes as you listen. How similar does it sound to a rainstorm or a gentle rain?

Check your rainstick for holes before you play and make sure it doesn't get wet. You can patch holes up with tape.

Use your rainstick whenever you want to practice mindfulness or calm down.

Cicadas

Find a comfortable seat. Rest your hands on your knees or in your lap. Breathe in as you sit up nice and tall, roll your shoulders back, lift your chin a little and start the Calm Down Countdown.

Trace the path with your finger, breathing in with the purple numbers and out with the green numbers.

Breathe in... 10   8   6   4   2

Breathe out...   9   7   5   3   1

Cicadas are insects. There are 3,000 species of them, all of which fall into two groups: annual cicadas, which we see every year, and periodical cicadas, which only appear once a decade or so.

Did You Know?

At 120 decibels, the cicada's buzz is the loudest noise any insect can make—even louder than a rock concert!

Periodical means something that only happens once in a while (like gym period at school). The scientific name of these periodical cicadas is *Magicicada*. Look at how that's spelled—it has the word "magic" in it! This is fitting because the cicada's life cycle is pretty magical!

After hatching, periodical cicadas burrow into the earth to start their 13- or 17-year life underground. Scientists believe that because they all come out together in such a gigantic number, even if some are eaten, there will still be more than enough cicadas to mate and continue the life cycle of the species by laying more eggs.

And what are cicadas doing all that time underground? Well, they're actually very active, tunneling and feeding. They will drink liquids from tree roots, like sap. After the 13 or 17 years are up, the cicadas will all come up from the ground together and begin climbing up the same trees.

Why do most cicadas only come out of the ground after 13 or 17 years? Scientists think that over the years, cicadas evolved to have very long life cycles to avoid predators and survive.

Yoga Time

Let's pretend we have beautiful wings like a cicada.

1 Sit and bring the bottoms of your feet together with your knees out to the sides and your toes pointing forward.

2 Hold onto your feet and "flap" your wings up and down 10 times.

3 Keep going at your own pace and stop when you want to stop.

Mindful Moment

We're going to play a little mindfulness game now called Backbone Breathing!

Put your hand on your spine while you imagine a little toy car. What color is your car?

Pretend your car is parked on the lowest part of your backbone, in between your hips. **Breathe in.** As you inhale, imagine the toy car *slowly* driving up the backbone road along your spine.

Once the car gets to the top of your head, breathe out and picture it driving back down the way it came.

Try it again, and this time, try to breathe more *slowly* up and down. Let the little car enjoy the ride!

Cicada Art

Draw and color in your own cicada.

Mycelium Mindfulness

Let's start with the Calm Down Countdown.

Trace the path with your finger, breathing in with the purple numbers and out with the green numbers.

Breathe in...   10   8   6   4   2

Breathe out...   9   7   5   3   1

Many types of mushrooms have neat names, like enoki, saffron milk cap and turkey tail, to name a few! Mushrooms are part of the fungi family and start from spores (a cell that contains everything needed to form a new mushroom. Cells are very tiny and the only way we can see them is through a microscope). Spores float through the air and land on the ground or on trees and logs. After landing, they'll send out a little "stem" called a hypha (HI-fah). When one spore's hypha meets another spore's hypha, a new mushroom is created.

At the same time, they also begin making mycelium (my-SEE-lee-um) underground, which sort of looks like a small cotton ball that's been pulled apart, but if you look closer, they look like threads wrapped around tree roots. Mycelium gets nutrients from the soil or tree log to help it grow. Once it's ready, it'll create a "fruiting body"—the mushroom that we see above ground. These mushrooms then send out new spores to keep the life cycle going!

Mycelium's underground network connects trees and plants. Through this network, plant neighbors share nutrients and information. Trees can pass messages to each other, sending warning signals if there are pests in the area. It's the forest's version of the internet, and some people call it the wood wide web! Next time you're walking in the woods, take a look under a log. If you see some white patches, those might be mycelium!

Fun Fact
Underground mycelium networks can grow to be the size of an American football field!

Yoga Time

Do you know what infinity means? It means forever, never-ending. There's even a symbol for infinity: It looks like the number eight lying on its side.

1 Slowly trace an infinity symbol in the air with the tip of your nose.

2 Try making the symbol bigger. Take your time. You can imagine that your nose is a tiny spore floating back and forth through the air.

3 Feel the gentle stretches in your neck, but make sure you're not moving your neck too far or too fast. Relax.

4 Start to slow down your movement, and when your nose gets to the middle again, you can stop.

5 Try this in the other direction!

Mindful Moment

By practicing a loving kindness meditation, you can send kind wishes in your thoughts to people. Give yourself a hug if you like and say this to yourself:

May I be happy.
May I be healthy.
May I be safe.
May I live with ease.

(To live with ease doesn't mean life will always be easy, just that you're ready and able to deal with what life gives you.)

Next, choose someone you love and someone you may not be getting along with right now and think these thoughts to them. Repeat these phrases:

May you be happy.
May you be healthy.
May you be safe.
May you live with ease.

By focusing our thinking on positive, caring thoughts, our actions will line up. Let's send more kindness into the world whenever we can.

Thoughts Are Like Bubbles

Let's take a moment to slow down and do the Calm Down Countdown.

Trace the path with your finger, breathing in with the purple numbers and out with the green numbers.

Breathe in... 10   8   6   4   2

Breathe out...   9   7   5   3   1

Bubbles float through the air and you can't help but notice their rainbowy shine. Just like certain thoughts. Sometimes we have thoughts that make us feel anxious, which means they make us worry a lot. It's an uncomfortable feeling that might make it hard to concentrate or enjoy the things we are supposed to be doing, like paying attention in class, playing soccer with our friends or having dinner with our family. This feeling, called anxiety, stays with some of us longer than others.

Next time a thought that makes you feel anxious enters your head, just imagine it's a bubble. Bubbles don't last forever, and neither do thoughts!

FIGHT, FLIGHT OR FREEZE

When something stressful happens, your brain activates a response known as fight, flight or freeze mode. The part of your brain that does this is called the amygdala (uh-mig-duh-luh). Let's say you're playing baseball and see the ball flying at you...

FIGHT MODE: Taking action to stop the danger or stress.
EXAMPLE: You get into position and catch the baseball in your mitt.

FLIGHT MODE: Moving away from danger or stress
EXAMPLE: You duck out of the way.

FREEZE MODE: Pausing to figure out what you're going to do next.
EXAMPLE: You freeze, but at the last second, a friend catches the ball.

It's not healthy to always be in fight, flight or freeze mode, though. Once we recognize the feeling and see there's nothing we need to fight, run from or hide from, we can take the next healthy step forward.

Yoga Time

It's bubble time!

1 Reach your hands up in the air. How high can you stretch your fingertips up without your bottom leaving the ground?

2 Now touch your fingertips together to make a circle above your head. Let's pretend your circle is a bubble.

3 Take a deep breath in, then turn your belly button to face one side. Your bubble should be facing that side now, too.

4 Breathe out and move your bubble back to center.

5 Breathe in and turn your belly button to the other side.

6 Keep doing this at your own pace as many times as you'd like.

7 When you're done, shake out your arms and relax.

Mindful Moment

Give Me Five is a grounding activity to help you stay in the present moment. Mindfulness can help you find your calm when you start to feel anxious.

1. Take five deep breaths.
2. Focus on your five senses.

○ Start with a **thumbs** up! Name one thing you can see.

○ Now your **pointer finger.** Touch the tip of your pointer finger to your thumb, almost like you're making an OK sign. Because you're going to be OK. Name one thing in the room you can touch.

○ Touch your **middle finger** to your thumb and name something you can hear right now.

○ Bring your **ring finger** to your thumb. Name something you can smell now, or think of your favorite smell.

○ Last one: Touch your **pinky** to your thumb. Name something you can taste or think of something yummy you like to eat.

The Big Dipper

Breathe in...   10   8   6   4   2

Breathe out...   9   7   5   3   1

There are billions of stars across the dark sky.

Constellations are stars that humans have grouped together to create shapes or pictures. They help us recognize and find stars. Long ago, the stars helped people tell time at night and navigate while sailing the seas.

People have created stories, or myths, about the constellations to help explain things that happened in their daily lives.

Here are three myths about the Big Dipper.

Greek Mythology
The goddess Hera was taking revenge on her husband Zeus and

the maiden Callisto. She turned Callisto into a bear, and Callisto wandered for years until one day, her son Arcas found her...but he didn't know it was his mother because she was still in bear form! Arcas was about to use his spear against her when Zeus saved them by sending them both up to the sky where Callisto became the Great Bear (Ursa Major/ The Big Dipper) and Arcas became the Little Bear (Ursa Minor/The Little Dipper).

Hindu Mythology

In ancient India, the Mahabharata (one of the major epic stories) tells the story of seven sages. A sage was a very wise person. The myth said that these seven sages made the sun rise every day. These sages are the seven stars in the Big Dipper.

Mythology of the Mi'kmaq, an Indigenous group in the Canadian Atlantic provinces

As the bear begins to wake up from its long hibernation, it is seen by Chickadee. Chickadee decides they want to hunt the bear! But Chickadee is too small, so they call for others to help. Six other hunters join in: Robin, Pigeon, Saw-whet Owl, Barred Owl, Moosebird and Blue Jay. These seven animals are the seven stars in the Big Dipper.

Yoga Time

❶ Lay down on your back. Bring your knees up, feet on the floor.

❷ Pretend there is a pan on the ground in front of your feet, filled with glow-in-the-dark paint.

❸ Close your eyes and dip your toes into the paint.

❹ Lift both legs (or just one leg) in the air and start dotting the sky with your toes to make stars! Bring your feet (or foot) down again to get more paint and then keep painting the sky. (You can put your hands under your lower back to support it.)

❺ When you're done, stretch out your arms and legs. You can even imagine the beautiful night sky you've painted and admire your masterpiece!

❻ Repeat anytime you'd like.

Mindful Moment

Create your own constellation! Connect the stars in any order, as many or as few as you like. Give your constellation a name and tell a story about it.

My constellation is called

_____

_____

_____

_____

_____

Here Be Dragons

ROAR! Try doing the Calm Down Countdown like a dragon today: Breathe in with the purple numbers and **ROAR** at the green numbers.

Breathe in... 10   8   6   4   2

Breathe out...   9   7   5   3   1

Dragons are mythical creatures that have appeared as myths in different cultures from almost every continent: Asia, Europe, the Americas and Australia. Many people have been fascinated by the idea of dragons—they're mysterious, powerful and just cool!

The idea of dragons may have come from ancient people discovering dinosaur bones and imagining the huge ferocious creatures they may have belonged to. An anthropologist (ann-throw-PAH-luh-gist) is someone who studies humans from the past and present. One anthropologist named David Jones thought the idea of dragons came from our natural fear of predators, which may have helped build up the dragon mythology through the ages. If this is true, it wouldn't be a surprise.

It's natural for us to be afraid, and the unknown can be especially scary. The unknown usually comes with change and that can all feel out of our control. This is natural and part of being human! Our ancestors from long ago had to work hard to survive and moved around to look for water, food and shelter. Relocating from one place to another could have meant losing out on access to one (or more!) of these necessities, so over time it became natural for humans to want to avoid change.

But that doesn't mean change is bad! We can embrace it.

Fun Fact

Mapmakers used to draw monsters and other imaginary creatures on areas that hadn't yet been explored. One 16th-century globe marked these areas with the phrase "Here be dragons" in Latin.

Yoga Time

Let's do the dragon pose.

1 Start on your hands and knees.

2 Step your right foot between your hands. Make sure your knee is above your heel.

3 Gently slide your left leg back and press the top of your foot against the floor as shown so there is less weight on your knee. You can also put a towel or blanket under your knee for support.

4 Breathe in and out five times.

5 When you're ready, step your right foot back.

Try this again, but this time, step your left foot between your hands and stretch out your right leg.

Mindful Moment

Change and the unknown don't have to be scary. They can even be exciting and fun! Next time you're facing change, try one of these ideas:

• **Think back** to when you were in a similar situation and how you handled it. Did it go well? Is there anything you would do differently?

• **Talk to someone you trust** about it. People who love and support you can share ideas or be a listening ear.

• **Pay attention** to how characters in books and movies handle stress. What worked out well? Would it work for you? What would you do differently?

• **Do a trial run** before you try something new. It might help take away some of the worry if you have an idea of what to expect and have a chance to practice.

• **And...YET.** Instead of thinking you can't do something, add the word "yet": "I can't do that...yet." "It doesn't work...yet." "I'm not good at this...YET." By adding the "yet," you're reminding yourself that you are always learning and that it takes time. And that's a good thing! It's fun to learn and gain new skills. Keep at it!

Anger

ARGH! What do you do when you feel angry? What happens in our brains and bodies when we're upset? Let's do the Calm Down Countdown first so we can start off in a relaxed place. Trace the path with your finger, breathing in with the purple numbers and out with the green numbers.

Breathe in...   10   8   6   4   2

Breathe out...   9   7   5   3   1

Picture a fire station. Red helmets and big boots lined up in neat rows along one wall. Bright red fire trucks.

Suddenly, the fire alarm goes off! Firefighters slide down the pole, pull on boots and helmets and hop into the trucks. Everyone knows their job and exactly what to do.

Our brains and bodies are like firefighters when something stresses us out. They jump into action and go into fight, flight or freeze mode (read more about this on pg. 41). When we get angry, we can feel it:

☑ Your face might turn red and feel warm (your blood vessels widen and your blood flow increases)

☑ Your heart beats faster

☑ You might grind your teeth

☑ You might clench your fists

☑ You might feel shaky

☑ Your pupils grow larger

It's NOT easy to remember to take a moment to breathe when things are difficult and you feel angry. This is difficult for grown-ups, too! That's why it's good to practice pausing every day when you are already calm.
This way, your brain and body will get into the habit of pausing before you get to the point when it's hard to settle down.

Yoga Time

What You Need
Pillow or cushion

Try this while sitting cross-legged on a cushion or pillow.

❶ Move closer to the edge of the pillow. Cross your legs.

❷ Rest your hands in your lap or the tops of your thighs.

❸ Sit up tall. Roll your shoulders back. You can close your eyes.

❹ Take three to five deep breaths in and out (or as many as you'd like). Relax.

Give this a try any time you'd like a chance to calm down. This sitting pose helps your body relax by starting up the parasympathetic (peh-rah-sim-pah-THEH-tik) nervous system. This relaxes your body after stress by slowing down your breathing and heart rate, which in turn lowers your blood pressure.

This is always good, but it's especially helpful after you've been feeling angry or stressed.

Mindful Moment

FIND YOUR OWN MINDFUL MOMENT

Choose a time of day to press pause on life, even for a minute. If you keep doing this every day at the same time, it'll become a habit, something you do without thinking. See which one works best for you!

• **Do the Calm Down Countdown.** Count down from 10 while taking deep breaths in through your nose and out through your mouth.

• **Go for a walk.** Try to spot at least one thing from each color of the rainbow!

• **Listen to nature.** Open a window or go outside. Sit for a few minutes and close your eyes if you'd like. How many different sounds can you hear?

• **Try "easy breezy lemon squeezy."** Squeeze your fists as tight as you can for five seconds. Then slowly release and relax. Do it again and focus on the difference in how your hands feel before and after.

Super Star Fruit!

Trace the path with your finger, breathing in with the purple numbers and out with the green numbers.

Breathe in... 10   8   6   4   2

Breathe out...   9   7   5   3   1

Is there a fruit that looks cooler than the star fruit? When you cut it open, it's in the shape of a perfect star! Native to Southeast Asia, this tasty treat is grown in different tropical areas and enjoyed all over the world!

The skin is a waxy green or yellow color and can be eaten too. When ripe, the star fruit is crunchy, juicy and sweet (with a slight tart or sour taste to it).

Star fruit is very nutritious because it contains a lot of vitamin C and B5, fiber, protein, folate and more! In some countries, people will even eat star fruit to help them feel better when they are sick.

Even though star fruit can make for a very healthy snack, it can affect some people negatively. Trying new things is great and makes life fun, but it's a good idea to check with a grown-up you trust if you're not sure about something.

What was the last new food you tried? What did you think of it? Did you know that sometimes it takes our taste buds a few tries before they become used to a certain flavor? If there's a food you've tried and weren't sure about it (and you weren't allergic to it), give it another chance! You might end up loving it.

Yoga Time

MIRROR ME

You'll need to really concentrate for this yoga game!

What You Need A partner (a grown-up, your brother or sister or a friend)

❶ You and your partner should sit facing each other. Choose who will be the mirror and who will be the STAR!

❷ The star looks at the mirror and slowly begins to move. The mirror's job is to watch closely and copy their movements.

❸ When you're ready, switch roles.

A twist to this game: Sit behind your partner. Your partner can close their eyes as you draw a shape or trace a letter on their back and ask them to guess what it is. After a few shapes, switch roles.

Mindful Moment

LUCKY STAR ORIGAMI

Send kind wishes to others with one of these stars.

What You Need
• A ½"-by-11" strip of colorful A4 paper (cut from the long side of the paper)

① At one end of the strip, tie a simple overhand knot.

② Tuck the short end into one of the folds.

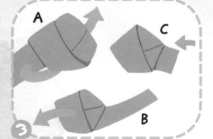

③ Wrap the long end of the paper strip behind your knot so the end is pointing to the right, then fold the strip in front of the knot to the left (A). Continue wrapping (B). When you get to the end, tuck the end into one of the folds (C).

④ Gently pinch the corners to make your star puff up.

Cave of Wonders

Have you ever been inside a cave? Caves are interesting and fun to explore, and sometimes they hold a secret or two! Before we go exploring, let's take a few deep breaths together with the Calm Down Countdown.

Trace the path with your finger, breathing in with the purple numbers and out with the green numbers.

Breathe in...   10   8   6   4   2

Breathe out...   9   7   5   3   1

A cave is a natural hole in the earth that is big enough for a human to fit inside. Most caves are formed when acidic water slowly breaks down karst, which is land made of limestone. Limestone is soft rock that can be dissolved in acidic water. As karst breaks down, the leftover space becomes a cave.

Caves can be small with passages so narrow you have to crawl to get through.

Some caves are enormous and have their own waterfalls and lakes, like the Mammoth Cave in Kentucky.

Other caves are famous for their beautiful scenery, like the Blue Grotto on the island of Capri. It is known for its gorgeous turquoise-blue water.

Caves also have rock formations, including stalactites and stalagmites. On the next page, let's pretend to grow tall like a stalagmite.

Did You Know?

The biggest cave in the world is in Vietnam. The Hang Son Doong ("Mountain River Cave") measures more than 1 billion cubic feet (or over 38 million cubic meters) in volume. That's one big cave!

Yoga Time

1. Stand up.

2. Put your hands on your hips.

3. Bring your right knee up to your chest and hug it with your right arm.

4. When you feel balanced, reach your left arm up to the sky.

5. Take three deep breaths in and out.

6. Slowly put your foot down.

7. Shake out your arms and legs, then try it on the other foot.

8. Repeat as many times as you'd like. Try balancing for a little longer if you want a challenge!

Mindful Moment

Look at this picture of a cave for 30 seconds. Next, look away and try to name as many things as you can. Can you remember at least 5 items in the picture?

How many things did you remember? Try again to see if you can name more, or make it more challenging by looking at it for less time.

What's in the Cave?
See how many items you can spot!

Salmon Run Home

Let's calm down with the Calm Down Countdown.

Trace the path with your finger, breathing in with the purple numbers and out with the green numbers.

Breathe in...   10   8   6   4   2

Breathe out...   9   7   5   3   1

Salmon go through a lot of stages of growth, and each stage has its own name: Alevins, Fry, Parr, Smolt and then the adult stage when they are all grown up. They begin life as an egg in a riverbed. The female salmon uses her tail to dig a hole in the riverbed's gravel in which to lay her eggs.

When little salmon are a year old, they reach the Parr stage, when they're about the length of a crayon. They will live in freshwater rivers for one to five years.

Salmon have a superpower: a homing instinct. That means they can find their way home even from very far away. Salmon can return to the exact river where they were born, even if they travel as far as 2,000 miles (about 3,000 km) away!

Salmon navigate back to their home rivers by using their super sense of smell and the earth's magnetic field. As they swim upstream, they jump over waterfalls and swim against the current (the flow of water). Every year, many people keep track of this salmon "run" and will go to rivers to watch salmon jumping out of the water on their return trip home. If you live close to a river, ask a grown-up to see if there's a salmon run near you!

On the next page, we'll pretend to be a salmon leaping over the water to go home.

Yoga Time

1 Lay down on your belly.

2 Lift yourself up onto your elbows and hands. Make your arms straight so they look like the number 11.

3 Try to move your elbows until they are right under your shoulders.

4 Rest here for five breaths in and out.

5 When you're done, slowly come back down to the ground and rest on one cheek.

6 Repeat the steps above, then end by resting on your other cheek.

Mindful Moment

Home looks different to all of us, and it can mean more than the four walls and roof around you. Your home can be a place, like a street, city or town, but it can also be a person or people (family or friends). Home is wherever, and with whomever, you feel happy, safe and loved.

Where or who is your home? Picture those things in your mind right now. What do you see? How does that place or person make you feel? Draw and color in your thoughts below. Feel free to add your own designs and drawings that represent home to you!

My home looks like...

Kelp Helps

Start with the Calm Down Countdown.

Trace the path with your finger, breathing in with the blue numbers and out with the yellow numbers.

Breathe in... 10   8   6   4   2

Breathe out...   9   7   5   3   1

We're in a shallow part of the ocean now because that's where kelp grows. Kelp is a large, brown algae seaweed. You might think of kelp as a plant (I always did!), but it's actually part of the protist kingdom and is a multi-cellular organism. It does, however, share some similarities to plants because it has what look like stems, roots and leaves.

Kelp forests cover one-quarter of the coasts around the world! Fish use them as nurseries for their eggs while seabirds, sea lions and sea otters take shelter in kelp forests to hide from predators and stay safe during storms.

Did You Know?

Sea otters wrap themselves in giant kelp so that they don't float away while they're sleeping!

Some kelp can grow up to 100 feet (about 30 meters) tall! That's why kelp forests are also called the "sequoias of the sea." Do you know what a sequoia is? They're huge redwood trees and, like all other trees, they help clean the air by breathing in carbon dioxide and breathing out fresh, clean oxygen. Kelp forests do the same good work by sucking up the carbon to help clean the air.

Sea creatures aren't the only ones that use this algae: Humans use giant kelp, too. For example, would you believe that you may have eaten something with kelp in it today? Did you have cereal this morning? Brush your teeth? Have yogurt or ice cream for dessert? Then you likely ate some kelp! Giant kelp is used to hold together or thicken things like cereal, toothpaste, yogurt, ranch dressing, lotion and, yes, ice cream!

Kelp forests are so useful and important to life on Earth. Kelp helps!

Yoga Time

1 Start on your hands and knees.

2 Stretch your right arm straight out ahead of you.

3 Keep your arm straight as you stretch out your left leg behind you.

4 Pretend your arm and leg make up a piece of giant kelp! Try stretching so it grows a little longer.

5 Bring your arm and knee back down on the ground. Try doing this on the other side.

6 Repeat as many times as you'd like.

Mindful Moment

Let's do a breathing exercise. While kelp forests breathe in carbon and breathe out oxygen, we do the opposite: We breathe in oxygen and breathe out carbon dioxide.

1 Trace the square, starting at any corner. Breathe in as you trace across and breathe out as you trace up and down. You can try holding your breath for a second or two when you reach the corners.

2 Go around the square slowly, enjoying your breathing.

3 Repeat as many times as you'd like. Come back to this page anytime you want to slow down.

Picasso Moth

Imagine your finger is a beautiful moth or butterfly flying up and down. Trace the path with your finger, breathing in with the purple numbers and out with the green numbers.

Breathe in...   10   8   6   4   2

Breathe out...   9   7   5   3   1

The Picasso moth is named after the famous artist Pablo Picasso!

Picasso, tell us, what's the difference between a moth and a butterfly?

PICASSO: A butterfly's antennae are mostly thin with small balls or bumps at the ends, whereas moths' antennae are feathery and don't have a bump at the end.

That's a great tip. How many moths are there in the world, and where do you live?

PICASSO: Hmm, I'm not sure, but I do know there are far more moths in the world than butterflies—if there were only 10 moths and butterflies in the whole world, nine of them would be moths and one would be a butterfly. Picasso moths live in parts of Asia and India. Here's one more interesting fact about us: Male moths have a super sense of smell and use their antennae to grab scent molecules in the air. One scientist tested this and found one moth could smell something from 23 miles (37 kilometers) away!

Wow! Thanks for all the fun facts, Picasso!

Did You Know?

Moths and butterflies are part of the same group of insects called Lepidoptera (leh-pih-DOP-ter-uh).

Yoga Time

Let's try something different! We can live mindfully in so many ways, including by dancing!

1 Clear some space in the room.

2 Put on some music.

3 Listen to the music. Find the beat. Move carefully and thoughtfully around the room.

4 When you're ready to stop, slow down and strike one last pose!

Mindful Moment

A drawing of a tree is a drawing of a tree. But if you see a painting full of dots, lines and splashes of different colors, what is it a painting of?

Abstract art can be seen differently by different people. Everyone who sees it might have their own feeling or reaction, which might not all be the same.

Picasso was an abstract artist, and his art makes people feel different things. One of the best things about art is that it lets us express (or let out) our feelings in a healthy way.

Try expressing each of these emotions through art. You could paint or draw sadness, dance happiness or even act out disgust. Mix them up! Challenge a friend or family member to do the same.

Happy

Sad

Surprised

Disgusted

Excited

Curious

Mother Earth's Magic Light Show

Have you ever heard of the northern lights? These colorful lights appear in the night sky in different places around the world, such as Iceland or the Yukon in Canada. The northern lights are also called the aurora borealis (uh-ROR-ruh bor-ree-AL-iss).

Why and when do these beautiful lights appear? What causes them? Scientists have an answer! These green, blue, pink and purple streaks of light are caused by tiny particles called electrons being blown by solar winds, which are winds from the sun. When these electrons come into the earth's atmosphere, they mix with various gasses and begin to glow! Different gasses make different colors:

Oxygen = green and red

Hydrogen and Helium = purple and blue

Nitrogen = pink and dark red

But before scientists discovered the answer, humans tried to explain the aurora borealis, passing down stories about their origins to their children. From the beginning of time, humans have been telling stories to help make meaning of what is happening around them.

The first story is from the Vikings! The Valkyries were said to be immortal female warriors who brought the other warriors to Valhalla, a place where heroes' souls live forever. The Vikings believed the lights in the sky were the reflections of the Valkyries' shields and armor.

Another legend about the aurora borealis comes from China. Early legends suggest the northern lights are actually the fire from good and evil dragons battling in the sky!

There are many North American Indigenous groups and many legends about the northern lights, including one that posits the lights are the spirits of the animals they hunted.

Yoga Time

❶ Sit in a way that is comfortable for you. Think about where your belly button is pointing right now (straight ahead).

❷ Take a deep breath in and sit up taller.

❸ Breathe out and slowly twist your belly button to the right so it's pointing that way. You can rest your hands on your knees or on the floor.

❹ Breathe in again and come back to center.

❺ Breathe out and slowly twist your belly button to the left. Rest your hands on your knees or on the floor.

❻ Breathe in and come back to center.

Repeat as many times as you want, moving slowly.

Mindful Moment

You know when you see someone doing something they love, something they're great at, something they work hard for and they seem so...happy? Excited? Almost like they're...glowing? Have you figured out what you're good at or what you love to do? This can be tough sometimes, but asking your teacher or parent or someone else you trust can help! Once you know, try to find a way to use that special talent and ability to do something kind for someone. Remember: A candle doesn't lose anything by sharing its flame!

Make a list of the things you like to do and things you're good at (these can be the same thing).

What do you like to do?

Dugongs

Dugongs are gentle giants that look sort of like giant walruses, with big gray bodies and round, flattish snouts. They can grow as long as 13 feet (4 meters) and weigh more than 800 pounds (360 kilograms)! They reside in the Indian and western Pacific Oceans and can live up to 70 years. The largest group of dugongs lives in Australian waters, a group of more than 80,000 animals!

Dugongs are related to manatees and their ancestors are land animals, so some scientists think dugongs may be more closely related to elephants than whales!

Dugongs are also called sea cows. Why do you think they're called sea cows? Dugongs are the only marine animals that are herbivores (animals that only eat plants). While cows on land graze on grass, the dugong grazes on grass growing on the ocean floor.

Dugongs don't have any natural predators. However, they are still in danger because of humans. Sometimes they accidentally get caught in fishing nets. And their habitat is being destroyed whenever humans build on the land by the sea, damaging the seabed.

Did You Know?

You may already know that we can tell how old a tree is by counting the number of rings around its trunk. You can also tell how old a dugong is by counting the number of rings around its tusks!

What can we do to help? We need to make sure when we are building and changing the land around us that we are very careful and mindful of the environment and think about how our actions affect others, including plants and animals. Next time you're playing outside and notice an insect, snail or worm on the ground, try to play around it or even just stop and watch it. It will not hurt you.

You can always go around and choose not to hurt them, and you might learn something new from observing them too.

Yoga Time

Sit and stretch your legs straight out in front of you. Now bring your legs out into a V with your feet as far apart as is comfortable. Close your eyes if you'd like. Imagine you're a dugong and right in front of you is a patch of yummy seagrass!

❶ Take a deep breath in and stretch your arms up above your head, wave your hands a little...and then stretch forward until they touch the ground. You can pretend to eat some seagrass too. If you need to, you can bend your knees a little or bring your legs a little closer together.

❷ Breathe in and stretch your fingers forward...then breathe out and bring your hands to the ground (and get more yummy seagrass). Let's do that again: Breathe in, stretch forward, breathe out and come closer to the ground. Great!

3 Walk your hands slowly backward, lifting yourself back up to a seated position. We can have another little stretch by putting our hands on the floor behind us and looking up to the sky. Come back when you're ready.

Repeat as many times as you like.

Mindful Moment

Dugongs can't see very well, but they have incredible hearing. They communicate with each other using chirps, barks, squeaks and other sounds underwater, just like dolphins. Let's focus on our sense of hearing right now. You're going to hold up a fist and spend 10 seconds just listening to the sounds around you. Every time you hear a sound, keep track by holding up a finger. You can close your eyes if you'd like and start now!

How many sounds did you hear?

You can try this mindful listening game anytime and see if you can hear more sounds each time.

Gratitude Attitude

Trace the path with your finger, breathing in with the purple numbers and out with the green numbers.

Breathe in... 10   8   6   4   2

Breathe out...   9   7   5   3   1

Being grateful means appreciating what we have. That includes physical things and emotional things. Why is it important to be grateful? Practicing gratitude helps us remember there's lots of good stuff and good people in the world.

It's also healthy for you for so many other reasons. Gratitude can:

• Improve your attention, energy and determination

• Make you feel more optimistic

• Boost positive feelings

• Lessen aches and pains

• Improve your sleep

• Lessen feelings of anxiety and depression

When we practice gratitude, it changes our brains! Researchers have found that when people feel grateful, the areas of the brain in charge of empathy become more active! Gratitude keeps us healthy and makes us feel good, too.

Yoga Time

1 Stand with your feet wide.

2 Bend your knees and reach for the ground. Bring your bottom down, close to the floor.

3 Press your hands together in front of your heart. Rest your elbows against the inside of your knees. Count to 10.

4 When you're done, put your hands on the floor for balance as you come out of this pose.

Mindful Moment

GRATITUDE JOURNAL
Every day, write something or someone you feel grateful for on this list. Start right now. It can be

anything, like "comfy PJs" or "my pet turtle" or "pizza days." It can be just one word or two or three.

Then, tomorrow, write something else down. And keep going every day until you fill up this list!

FIRST WEEK	SECOND WEEK	THIRD WEEK	FOURTH WEEK
DAY 1	DAY 1	DAY 1	DAY 1
DAY 2	DAY 2	DAY 2	DAY 2
DAY 3	DAY 3	DAY 3	DAY 3
DAY 4	DAY 4	DAY 4	DAY 4
DAY 5	DAY 5	DAY 5	DAY 5
DAY 6	DAY 6	DAY 6	DAY 6
DAY 7	DAY 7	DAY 7	DAY 7

Once you're done, you can use a small notebook to keep up your one-word gratitude journal.

Fit as a Fiddlehead

A fiddlehead is the coiled tip of a plant called the ostrich fern and is—wait for it—older than dinosaurs! Fossils of tree ferns show that they have been around for more than 100 million years, twice as long as dinosaurs. Wow!

Before we learn more about these intriguing plants, let's relax with the Calm Down Countdown:

Trace the path with your finger, breathing in with the purple numbers and out with the green numbers.

Breathe in... 10   8   6   4   2

Breathe out...   9   7   5   3   1

Fiddleheads can grow very tall, as tall as a person! You can also find them in grocery stores or at the farmer's market in the springtime.

These plants are very nutritious and healthy—they're full of potassium, vitamin A (which makes them good for your eyes and immune system, keeping you healthy) and C (which helps keep your muscles, blood and bones strong). Fiddleheads are delicious and nutritious but have to be boiled for 15 minutes before you can eat them safely.

Fiddleheads got their name because they look like the curled part at the top of a fiddle or violin (which is called a scroll). You can find spiral shapes everywhere in nature, from pine cones to sunflowers to shells and even galaxies! When plants grow in a spiral shape, they take up less space and grow tighter together, making them stronger. This helps them stand up to harsh weather.

On the next page, let's pretend we're a fiddlehead unfurling.

Fun Fact
The village of Tide Head in New Brunswick is known as the Fiddlehead Capital of the World!

Yoga Time

1 Take a moment to feel your spine (backbone), which is made up of stacked vertebrae. It starts between your hips and goes all the way up your back to between your ears!

2 Stand up (or sit down).

3 Bow forward all the way, then touch the ground.

4 Imagine that each vertebra is a block and you're stacking them up to make a tall tower. Slowly roll up until you're sitting up straight.

When you're finished, you can bow forward and try it again, breathing out as you fold down and breathing in slowly as you roll up.

Mindful Moment

Fiddleheads are spiral-shaped. Spirals go so well with mindfulness because they're a natural shape that grows, which is what we want to do. A spiral radiates out from its center but also comes back into itself.

It's so important to pause during the day to check back in with ourselves and ask: How am I feeling right now? Do I want to do something about how I'm feeling? Do I need help with anything? Do I need to take a break? Taking a moment to pause can help us mentally recharge so we're ready for whatever's next.

❶ Take a pause now. Breathe in and slowly trace the spiral starting at the outer end and going all the way to the center.

❷ Then, breathe out as you go back and trace your way out of the spiral.

❸ Try this a few more times. When you're ready to stop, check in to see how you're feeling.

Come back to this page any time you want to do spiral breathing!

Geodes:
A Look Inside

You might think you know what's inside something based on what the outside looks like. But that's not always true. Believe it or not, things (and people) are not always what they seem.

That's especially true for geodes. Have you ever seen one? Geodes may look like plain round rocks from the outside, but inside, they're hollow and lined with minerals, including crystals. You may have seen big ones in stores or museums, and they are often cracked open and polished so you can examine their beautiful inner crystal layers.

Let's take a moment to pause. Sit up tall. Relax your back. Put your hands in your lap or on your knees. If you want, close your eyes (unless you're reading!).

Take a deep breath in through your nose...and breathe out through your nose...

Keep breathing like this as we do the Calm Down Countdown.

Trace the path with your finger, breathing in with the purple numbers and out with the green numbers.

Breathe in... 10   8   6   4   2

Breathe out...   9   7   5   3   1

Geodes are created when bubbles of air (called air pockets) get trapped inside the rock as it forms. Tiny drops of water—moisture from the soil or other rocks—slowly find their way into these air pockets. The water eventually evaporates and leaves behind the minerals it had been carrying. This process happens again and again over THOUSANDS of years. The minerals gradually build up until the crystals have filled up the air pocket in the rock.

Remember, a geode may look plain on the outside, but once it's opened, you reveal the beautiful, glittering minerals and crystals inside. Each geode grows its crystals in different patterns, shapes and sizes based on the environment in which it forms. No two are exactly alike—each one is as special and unique as you are.

Yoga Time

Let's dig for geodes!

1 Stretch out your legs so that they form a "V" shape.

2 Pick up one of your feet with both hands, holding it close to your stomach. Pretend your foot is a shovel and let's dig for some geodes!

3 Switch legs. Pick up your other foot, oops, I mean shovel. Dig with your new shovel.

4 Great work, we found something! Stretch both legs out now in that "V" shape again. Give them a wiggle.

5 Now, sit up tall again, reach your arms over your head and lean forward, stretching your fingertips forward. Dig one more time with your hands.

6 Walk your hands back toward you and sit back up.

7 Put down your geode somewhere safe.

Try digging for geodes again soon!

Mindful Moment

Have you ever heard the saying, "Don't judge a book by its cover"? It means you can't always tell what something or someone is like just by looking at them. You have to read the book or spend time with the person to get to know them.

Think about a time when you thought one way about someone or something but things turned out better than you expected. What did you think would happen, and what actually happened? What do you think you'll remember about this situation? Draw or write about it below. If you ever feel broken or not good, remember that everyone is always growing and will become a crystal in their own time.

Sea Bunny

It's time to meet one of the cutest critters in the sea.

Let's dive right in with the Calm Down Countdown!

Trace the path with your finger, breathing in with the purple numbers and out with the green numbers.

Breathe in...   10   8   6   4   2

Breathe out...   9   7   5   3   1

Imagine you're swimming underwater, deep in the big, blue, beautiful waters of the Indo-Pacific region, which is made up of part of the Indian Ocean and part of the Pacific. We're near the equator, in Earth's warmest ocean water.

Jorunna parva, or sea bunnies, look like they are

fluffy, but if you take a closer look, you can see they actually have tiny little rods all over their bodies. They even have what look like bunny ears! These are called rhinophores and they're a sensory organ that can detect chemicals in the water. This helps the sea bunnies find food and mates.

Despite their name, sea bunnies aren't related to rabbits—they're sea slugs, which are part of the mollusk family. These critters are invertebrates (in-VER-tuh-brits), meaning they have no backbone. Unlike slugs, humans have backbones (spines), which makes us vertebrates (VER-tuh-brits). Invertebrates = no backbone, vertebrates = backbone.

All animals have ways of protecting themselves from predators. Sea bunnies only live for a few months to a year. Because they're poisonous, not a lot of predators will try to eat them so they stay fairly safe. Feeling safe feels nice. Let's do a pose together that some people like because they feel safe in it and many people also like because it feels calming: It's called Child's Pose!

Yoga Time

1 Sit on your knees and put your hands out in front of you on the ground.

2 Bow forward and rest your forehead on the floor. (You can also make two fists and stack them on top of each other and rest your forehead on top or bring your knees wide if that feels more comfortable.)

3 Close your eyes if you want to and breathe here for as long as you'd like.

4 When you're ready, slowly roll over to one side and then onto your back.

5 Hug your knees to your chest, then slowly roll back and forth to give your back a massage.

Mindful Moment

Sea bunnies live in warm waters. Let's warm up, too!

1 Start rubbing your hands together...a little faster... and just a little faster....

2 Gently place your hands on your cheeks.

3 Focus on the warmth from your hands transferring to your cheeks.

4 Cup your hands over your eyes.

5 Take a deep breath in...and let it out.

Things That Make Me Feel Safe
Draw or write about things that make you feel warm and fuzzy or protected.

Fine and Dandy

Trace the path with your finger, breathing in with the purple numbers and out with the green numbers.

Breathe in...   10   8   6   4   2

Breathe out...   9   7   5   3   1

Dandelions are sometimes called weeds, but they're actually helpful flowers. Their cheery faces tell us spring is here. Every part of a dandelion can be used, from the roots to the leaves. Dandelions can be eaten in a salad, and you can make dandelion tea and jam. People have also used these flowers to make food dye and medicine.

Dandelions provide nectar for butterflies and other insects. They are one of the first plants to grow back after a wildfire. Dandelion roots help hold soil together so it doesn't erode. What great little helpers!

During their life cycle, each stage looks like a different celestial (suh-LES-tee-ull) body: sun, moon and stars. The dandelion's bright yellow petals look like the shining sun. When the petals dry out and fall off, the white fluffy seeds create a puffy ball that looks like a full moon.

As the seeds blow away, they look like stars in the sky!

Yoga Time

1 Stand up.

2 Bring your feet out wide, toes facing out.

3 Bring your arms out to the sides. Bend at the elbow, palms facing up.

4 Bend your knees and pretend you're sitting on top of a box. You can close your eyes and breathe.

5 When you're ready, straighten your legs and bring your feet together.

6 Shake out your arms and legs and then try it one more time.

Mindful Moment

DANDELION BREATHING

1 Hold up your hand and pretend it's a fluffy white dandelion.

2 Take a deep breath in, then blow the dandelion fluff away!

3 Try again, this time taking a longer breath in so you have more breath to blow out.

4 One more time, except this time, you have a new full and fluffy dandelion and you're going to try to blow every single seed away!

Jackfruit
of All Trades

Trace the path with your finger, breathing in with the purple numbers and out with the green numbers.

Breathe in... 10   8   6   4   2

Breathe out...   9   7   5   3   1

All hail the mighty jackfruit! Wearing its spiky exterior like a crown, this fruit can do it all. Jackfruits are packed with protein (which helps you grow), fiber, vitamin C and other nutrients. People use them in sweet dishes like ice cream and savory meals, too. You can even use it in the place of meat in some recipes.

Did You Know?

The jackfruit is the national fruit of Bangladesh and Sri Lanka!

Each jackfruit tree can produce up to 150 (or sometimes even more!) fruits each year. The jackfruit is the biggest fruit that grows on trees, and a single fruit can weigh more than 80 pounds (36 kilograms)! Good thing they grow on the tree's trunk!

The wood of these trees is strong and can be used to build many things. The bark can help sick people. It has an orange color, and this is used to dye monks' robes. Animals such as livestock eat the tree's leaves.

Yoga Time

❶ Start on your hands and knees with your hands under your shoulders.

❷ Step your feet back as shown, so that your back and legs make a straight line.

❸ Count for five breaths in and out.

❹ Slowly bring your knees to the floor.
Try it again, working up to 10 breaths.

Mindful Moment

Let's do more yoga now...hand yoga!

① Sit comfortably.

② Put your left hand in your lap, palm facing up.

③ Place your right hand on top of your left hand, palm facing up.

④ Line up your right fingers so they're laying on top of your left fingers.

⑤ Let your thumbs lightly touch.

⑥ Sit with your hands in this meditation mudra (pose) called dhyana (DYE-ann-a). Take a few deep breaths in and out. Close your eyes if you'd like.

This is a good hand yoga pose for when you're practicing mindful meditation at home.

Star Stuff

We're going to do the Calm Down Countdown.
Trace the path with your finger, breathing in with
the blue numbers and out with the green numbers.

Breathe in...   10   8   6   4   2

Breathe out...   9   7   5   3   1

Red giant stars are massive stars that can be up to
620 million miles (1 billion kilometers) across, and
100 to 1,000 times bigger than the sun! A red giant
can live for a few thousand years or even up to
a billion...but then it'll eventually start to shrink,
then collapse onto itself and become a supernova...
bursting with super bright light and dust and gas.

Scientists believe one of these supernova explosions
sparked the creation of our solar system, and life on
Earth. Every element in our bodies is from these red
giant stars. All that stardust that came from the red
giants traveled far through space and is now within
us. We are made of the same stuff that stars are
made of! How awesome is that?

You are a star.

You are connected to everyone else around you, everyone in your city, everyone in your country, everyone in the entire world. We are all made up of the same stuff! We're the same. Connected.

You are connected to the earth, each blade of grass, every insect, bird, horse, tree, flower, the stars across the universe...we are all living and breathing together, trying to make each day good, healthy and fun, and maybe even helping to make the lives of others good, healthy and fun, too.

This is why it's so important for us to be kind: what we do will affect someone else. Let's always remember how we're connected when we make choices about how we treat other people, animals and plants. Kindness counts.

"All of the rocky and metallic material we stand on, the iron in our blood, the calcium in our teeth, the carbon in our genes were produced billions of years ago in the interior of a red giant star. We are made of star-stuff."

—Carl Sagan, astronomer and planetary scientist

Yoga Time

One element that we find in the earth and in our bodies is carbon. Carbon is special because its atoms, the teeny tiny pieces that make up matter, can come together and form different things. If the carbon atoms form one way, you get a diamond. If the carbon atoms form another way, you get graphite. Do you know what's made of graphite? Pencil lead!

Let's pretend our legs are pencils.

❶ Lie down on the ground (or sit if you like).

❷ Lift one leg up in the air and point your toes toward the sky.

❸ Your toes are graphite, which makes up the tip of a pencil! Write your name in the sky.

❹ Switch legs. Write your name again, or maybe your last name, with your "pencil."

❺ Try it again, and this time, draw a picture of your favorite fruit, tree or flower, one leg at a time.

Mindful Moment

Think of something that makes you happy—your family, a pet, toy, your favorite TV show or book...

Once you have that happy thought in your mind, smile! Keep thinking about what makes you happy. Did you know that smiling—really, truly happy smiles—can make you feel less stressed? It's true! When we feel stress, it can raise our heart rates (when you feel your heart beating faster than needed). Scientists have found that when we use our smiling muscles, a signal is sent to our brains to create more "happy hormones" (endorphins) as a reward! And that makes us smile even more!

Come back to this exercise whenever you feel stress or could use a happy moment in your day.

Draw or write about what makes you happy here.

Tip of the Iceberg

BRRR! It's cold here in Antarctica! We're here to see the icebergs, but let's take a moment to breathe with the Calm Down Countdown.

Trace the path with your finger, breathing in with the purple numbers and out with the yellow numbers.

Breathe in... 10   8   6   4   2

Breathe out...   9   7   5   3   1

Icebergs are chunks of ice that float in open water. They have broken off glaciers or ice shelves. They can be as small as a car or as big as a small country!

There are special names for small icebergs. For example, bergy bits are icebergs that are about the size of a small house! The smallest icebergs are called growlers and are less than 3 feet (1 meter) tall. When they melt, they let out air trapped inside, which can make a noise that sounds like an animal growling!

Scientists study icebergs and glaciers because they give us information about the past and clues about our future. By examining the ice, scientists can tell us what type of animals lived there thousands of years ago. They can also discover what happened with our climate over the years. This data can help us understand patterns and have a better idea of what might happen with climate change in the future. That affects us all, no matter where we live, so it's a very important area of study.

Did You Know?

The largest iceberg in the world is called A-76. It is more than 100 miles long and is located in the Weddell Sea in Antarctica.

Yoga Time

1 Stand up.

2 Put your hands on your hips. Move your feet so they are right underneath your hips. That is what's called "hip-width."

3 Make your knees soft by bending them just a little.

4 Place your arms at your sides and open your palms to the front.

5 Gently roll your shoulders back and down.

6 Keep your chin up.

7 Breathe in and out a few times.

Mindful Moment

Emotions can be complicated, especially "big" emotions like anger, excitement or frustration. Sometimes we can only see the emotion we feel the most, like the tip of an iceberg. As you get older, you might feel different emotions at the same time. Being mindful can help you understand what's happening so you can do something helpful about it.

For example: If you feel angry and take time to work out your feelings, you might realize that you're also feeling jealous of your new baby brother or sister. Now that you understand why, you can do something about it, like tell your grown-up that you would like some "just you and me" time with them.

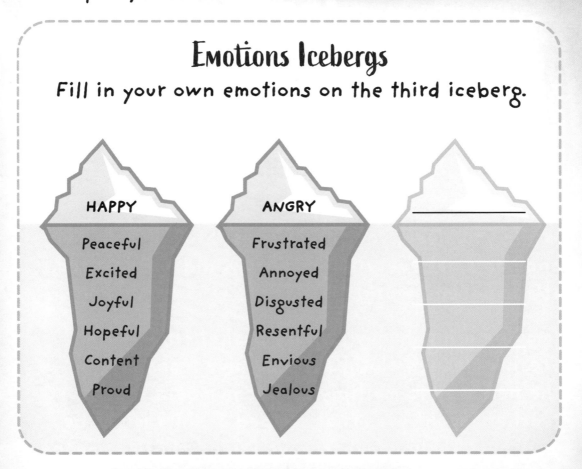

Emotions Icebergs

Fill in your own emotions on the third iceberg.

HAPPY	ANGRY	_____
Peaceful	Frustrated	
Excited	Annoyed	
Joyful	Disgusted	
Hopeful	Resentful	
Content	Envious	
Proud	Jealous	

Sleepyhead,
Ready for Bed

What are the necessities of life? What do we need to stay alive? Breathing, for sure. Water. Food. And there's one more thing...it's sleep! Human beings need sleep!

Let's slow down with the Calm Down Countdown. Trace the path with your finger, breathing in with the blue numbers and out with the green numbers.

Breathe in... 10   8   6   4   2

Breathe out...   9   7   5   3   1

While you sleep, your brain goes through your day and sorts out everything you saw, did and learned. It's important work!

Imagine a big, heavy laundry basket filled with freshly cleaned clothes. Those blue jeans may be the new way to multiply bigger numbers that your teacher taught you. That striped T-shirt might be your hurt feelings when your friend chose someone

else to sit beside
at lunch. The pink
sweater might be how
awesome you felt when you scored
your first goal in hockey!

Now, imagine dumping all the clothes
onto the floor. It's a messy, colorful jumble,
and it's a lot to take in all at once!

Just like you fold and put away your laundry,
your brain sorts through your day and puts
everything into neat, organized drawers
so that when you need to remember that
multiplication strategy or how good it felt
to score a goal, you can access those things
quickly and find what you need.

But if you don't get enough sleep, your
brain won't have time to properly sort and
put away your brain laundry. That's why
getting enough rest is so important!

Yoga Time

1 Lie down on your back (use a mat if you like).

2 Imagine you're a five-pointed star. Make a star shape with your arms and legs.

3 Take a deep breath in...then let it out.

4 Make your star shine by moving your arms and legs back and forth like you're making a snow angel.

5 When you're ready, come back to your star shape and take a few more deep breaths.

Mindful Moment

1 Have a seat or lie down.

2 Close your eyes. Breathe in and out. Make sure you're comfortable by checking in with your body.

3 Relax your face. Smooth your forehead and relax your eyes. Bring your bottom teeth away from your top teeth.

4 Roll your shoulders back. Make a fist and squeeze, tightening up your hand and arm muscles...and release.

5 Shake out your legs.

6 Wiggle your toes and move your feet in circles left or right, then switch directions.

7 Stay here and follow your breathing for as long as you like. Let your mind wander.

What's on Your Mind Today?
Draw or write about the brain laundry
you need to sort.

Lychee,
the Alligator Strawberry

Trace the path with your finger, breathing in with the purple numbers and out with the green numbers.

Breathe in... 10   8   6   4   2

Breathe out...   9   7   5   3   1

The lychee is a tropical fruit that grows on a tree. It can be pronounced LIE-chee or LEE-chee. Lychees are from China and are very popular there and in Southeast Asia.

Lychees have a bumpy, hard skin that looks and feels like a pink-red shell. They are ripe in late spring to summer but don't stay ripe very long. The inside of a lychee is white.

Did You Know?
Some people call the lychee the alligator strawberry. Why do you think that is?

Some people describe the taste as flowery or a cross between a strawberry and watermelon.

The lychee is a symbol of love. And you know who loves lychees?

Bees! Bees are attracted to the lychee's flowers, which are white, green or yellow and are fragrant (they smell sweet). Bees help pollinate lychee fruit. Honey made from lychee nectar is delicious.

Some call the lychee the Queen of Fruits because not only is it delicious, it's very nutritious, too! People like to eat them fresh and make them into juice, jelly, sweet sauces and more. Yum!

Yoga Time

1 Lie down on the floor.

2 Hug your knees to your chest.

3 Gently let go and let your knees fall to the left side.

4 Stretch your arms out to the sides.

5 Turn your head to the right.

6 Close your eyes and take a few deep breaths.

7 When you're ready, slowly bring your knees back to center. Hug them to your chest, let them fall to the right side and repeat.

Mindful Moment

TREE HUGGER

Next time you go outside, focus on your sense of touch. There are so many different textures in nature to explore (but if there's anything you're not sure of, ask a grown-up before touching it). Try the following and notice how each thing feels.

• Place your palm on the trunk of a tree (or hug it).

• Run your hands through the grass.

• Let sand fall through your fingers.

• Gently touch the petals of a flower.

• Hold a rock or pine cone in each hand. Would you be able to recognize which one is which without looking? (Don't forget to wash your hands afterward!)

There are so many things to explore outdoors and it's so good for you, too! Have fun!

Pebble Patience

We're going to do the Calm Down Countdown.

Trace the path with your finger, breathing in with the purple numbers and out with the green numbers.

Breathe in... 10   8   6   4   2

Breathe out...   9   7   5   3   1

Do you know the difference between a pebble and rock? Rocks are hard, solid and made of minerals. They have different shapes, colors and textures. Pebbles are much smaller than rocks and are usually round and smooth. How do pebbles get so smooth? By erosion!

Erosion is when something is worn down slowly, maybe by strong winds blowing or water moving over it again and again over many years.

In time, these forces change the shape of the pebble, smoothing out rough edges, until we are finally left with the round pebble we're now holding in our hands! You don't have to see something change to know that change happens.

Sometimes it's hard to be patient, to wait. If we're in line or waiting for something like our birthday or school holidays, it can feel like it's taking forever! And if we keep focusing on that event or thing we're excited about, we might forget to enjoy what's happening right now.

Change, or maybe having to be patient with others like younger siblings, can feel impossible, but it often just takes time. If a jagged, rough rock can transform into the smoothest beach pebble, we can change, too. And luckily, our changes don't take nearly as long, though it might not seem like it at the time. Next time you're waiting for something, take a few deep breaths and have the patience of a pebble!

Yoga Time

1 Lie down on the floor.

2 Bring your knees up and put your feet flat on the floor. Move your feet as close to your bottom as you can.

3 Palms of your hands are face down along your sides.

4 Take a deep breath in and lift your hips up to the sky!

5 You can close your eyes as you take five deep breaths in and out.

6 Slowly lower your bottom back on the ground.

7 Hug your knees to your chest. You can roll back and forth to give your back a massage.

8 If you want, try this again a few more times.

Mindful Moment

Let's practice something now that requires a lot of patience: sitting still. That could sound like the easiest thing in the world to you or it might seem like a challenge. But let's try it out for 15 seconds.

Close your eyes if they're not closed already. Sit up tall. Roll your shoulders back. Lift your chin up. You can put your hands in your lap or rest them on your knees. Take a deep breath in...then let it out.

Now, we sit. Just for a few moments. Start with 15 seconds here...go!

When you're done, use the chart below to track how you feel before and after meditating. Draw a face to show how you feel before you start and how you feel after you finish. Try doing this mindfulness activity every day and keep track of your feelings here.

☑ HINT
Try practicing this with a grown-up or a partner so you can help each other keep track of time.

	DAY 1	DAY 2	DAY 3	DAY 4	DAY 5	DAY 6	DAY 7
BEFORE SITTING How do I feel at this moment?							
AFTER SITTING How do I feel now?							

Capybaras
The Life of the Party!

What do you know about capybaras? Here are 10 fun facts about these fascinating creatures. Before we start, let's do the Calm Down Countdown.

Trace the path with your finger, breathing in with the purple numbers and out with the green numbers.

Breathe in... 10   8   6   4   2

Breathe out...   9   7   5   3   1

• Capybaras are friendly animals that love being around others. They live in groups of 10 to 20 ...even as many as 100!

• Sometimes you'll see birds hanging out on a capybara's back, helping pick off insects.

• Capybaras are related to guinea pigs.

• These animals are from South America.

• Capybaras can weigh more than 100 pounds (45 kilograms)!

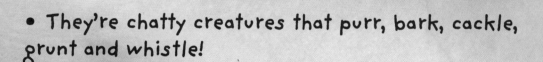

- They're chatty creatures that purr, bark, cackle, grunt and whistle!

- Capybaras can hold their breath underwater for up to five minutes!

- They live near water so they can go in to keep cool and hydrated as well as to escape predators.

- Their eyes and nose are closer to the top of their head so they can sneak a peek (and even sleep!) while in the water.

- Capybaras eat their own dung (that's poop!) in the mornings because it helps them digest more nutrients. (Another animal that does this? Rabbits!)

Share some of these animal fun facts with your family and friends!

Yoga Time

1 Lie down on your stomach.

2 Reach your arms out in front of you and point your toes.

3 Pretend to swim by kicking your feet and making big circles with your hands.

4 Try "swimming" for five breaths in and out.

5 When you're done, rest and then try again for 10 breaths!

How do you feel?

Mindful Moment

Draw your own capybara. Focus on the colors and lines as you go. Give them a name if you'd like!

My Capybara

Bamboo

Trace the path with your finger, breathing in with the purple numbers and out with the green numbers.

Breathe in...   10   8   6   4   2

Breathe out...   9   7   5   3   1

If you've ever looked at a bamboo forest, you might think it looks a lot like a tree forest, but bamboo is actually part of the grass family. Bamboo grows in warmer areas of the world such as Southeast Asia and islands in the Indian and Pacific oceans. There are more than 1,000 species of bamboo, some of which even grow in the southern United States.

Bamboo is one of the fastest-growing plants in the world. Some species can grow to be 130 feet (40 m) tall. That's taller than a 10-story building!

Bamboo is also special because it keeps our air clean by making more oxygen than trees!

Bamboo is used in many different ways. We can eat it, and farm animals can eat its leaves.
It's also the food of choice for pandas and red pandas, who love to eat the soft, tender shoots and leaves of the plant. Read more about red pandas on pg. 164.

Bamboo is strong and sturdy, which is why people use it to construct buildings and furniture. Its fiber is used to make clothing and it can replace plastic items like cutlery and toothbrushes. The plant's fast growth makes it an environmentally friendly option since it can be replaced quickly.

Yoga Time

1 Straighten your arm and lift it in front of you or *slightly* to the side.

2 Make a fist and keep your arm as straight and rigid as possible, like bamboo.

3 Focus on how your arm muscles feel right now, how tense they are.

4 Use your other hand and try pulling on that arm to test out how rigid it is. Can you move it or can you keep your arm stiff?

5 Now relax! Let your hand and arm go soft and loose. Shake out your arm and focus on how it feels now. Try it again with your other arm.

Mindful Moment

Bamboo can be used in so many ways. Being able to use something more than once or in the same fashion helps the planet. Can you think of other items in your home that you can use in different ways?

Choose one item. Make a list (or draw pictures) of as many ways it can be used or reused.

My Reusable Item

and all the ways it can be used...

T. Rex Twist!

The Tyrannosaurus rex was one of the largest carnivorous dinosaurs to ever roam the planet! It lived during a period called the Late Cretaceous (kre-TAY-shus) more than 65 million years ago.

Let's do the Calm Down Countdown to travel back in time! Trace the path with your finger, breathing in with the purple numbers and out with the green numbers.

Breathe in... 10   8   6   4   2

Breathe out...   9   7   5   3   1

The Tyrannosaurus rex is known for a few things, such as its big, strong tail! The tail helped the T. rex keep its balance and turn quickly as it chased after its prey.

Paleontologists (pay-lee-un-TAH-low-jists) are scientists who study dinosaurs. Some paleontologists believe the T. rex evolved to have smaller arms so the arms wouldn't get injured when these dinosaurs fed with their pack. They were able to do a lot with their super strong, sharp teeth and had a bite force (the pressure the teeth can take without breaking) of about 8,000 pounds! (Today, the strongest bite force champion is the saltwater crocodile, which has a bite force of 3,700 pounds or about half the bite force of the T. rex!)

With all that power in its jaws and teeth, it's no wonder the T. rex depended less on its arms than other animals!

Did You Know?

The name Tyrannosaurus rex means "king of the tyrant lizards."

Yoga Time

It's time to do the twist...the T. rex Twist, that is!

1 Take a deep breath in, turn to one side and let out a ROAR!

2 Breathe out and face forward again.

3 Breathe in, turn to the other side and...ROAR!

4 Breathe out and face forward.

5 Repeat each side three more times.

Well done! Your roars were ferocious!

Mindful Moment

One way to practice mindfulness is to build it into short, simple activities you already do every day. How about when you're brushing your teeth? Brushing your teeth is an important way to keep your teeth and gums clean, healthy and strong. After all, a great bite force depends on having strong teeth.

Next time you brush your teeth, focus on the action of brushing.

What does the brush feel like on your teeth? On your gums?*

Try closing your eyes (while you're over the sink!) and listen to the sound of the brushing.

Does your toothpaste have a flavor? Does it remind you of anything?

Does your toothpaste have a smell?

When you're done, give yourself a smile in the mirror. How would you describe your smile?

*Make sure you don't brush too hard!

The Sun Is a Star

Imagination is a superpower! Your imagination has no limits, just like outer space. So let's explore! Grab your space suit, hop into your spaceship and let's explore the universe, starting with the Calm Down Countdown!

Bring your attention to your breathing. Are you breathing quickly? Slowly? At your normal pace? Can you feel the air flow past your nostrils? When you breathe in, does your chest or tummy expand more?

Keep breathing in and out...and relax. Start at 10 and slowly breathe your way down to one.

Breathe in...   10   8   6   4   2

Breathe out...   9   7   5   3   1

The sun is a star and the largest body in our solar system. It's made up of hydrogen and helium, and its core is about 27 MILLION degrees Fahrenheit (or 15 MILLION degrees Celsius)! Why is the sun so important? Without the sun, life on our planet would be impossible for humans, animals, insects and even plants. The earth would be too cold! We need the sun's energy—its warmth and light—to survive. The sun is not just a star, it's *the* star of our universe!

The sun is so important that some ancient cultures even worshiped the sun! They built structures out of rock to track the sun's movement, chart the seasons and observe special sun events like solar eclipses. Why did they do all this? Because they knew how important the sun was to their lives. It's so important, some scientists specialize in heliophysics (hee-lee-oh-FIH-zicks), the study of the sun!

In yoga, sun salutations are a series of poses done facing the sun, a way of recognizing the role the sun has in our lives. Let's salute the sun together and show our gratitude by doing a version of sun salutations on the next page.

It would take 1.3 million Earths to fill the size of the sun!

Yoga Time

1 Sit up tall and press your hands together in front of your heart.

2 Breathe in and reach your hands up to the sky.

3 Breathe out and bring your hands to the floor. Look at your hands as you slide them forward, as far as you like.

4 Take another breath in and slide back and up, hands reaching for the sky again.

5 Breathe out and bring your hands to the floor again. Look at them as you slide forward.

6 Breathe in and slide back and up.

7 Keep going if you'd like, following your own breathing.

8 When you're ready to stop, bring your palms together in front of your heart. You can even say "thank you" out loud to the sun now to show your gratitude for making all life on Earth possible.

Mindful Moment

When planets, stars and even spacecraft move in a curved line around another object in space (such as the sun or a moon), this path is called an orbit. The curved path makes a shape called an ellipse.

It takes 365 days for the earth to complete an orbit all the way around the sun, which is why there are 365 days in a year. That means every time you celebrate a birthday, you're also celebrating that the earth, with you on it, has traveled all the way around the sun!

Trace the orbit line above. How old are you? Trace the ellipse that many times to represent how many times YOU have traveled around the sun already for each year of your life. You can use your finger or different colored pencils or crayons to note the path.

A Breath of
Fresh (Sea) Air!

You may already know trees help clean the earth's air, but there is another, much larger natural air purifier out there: the Barents Sea!

Before we dive in, why don't we slow down and settle in with the Calm Down Countdown?

Trace the path with your finger, breathing in with the purple numbers and out with the yellow numbers.

Breathe in...   10   8   6   4   2

Breathe out...   9   7   5   3   1

The Barents Sea is part of the Arctic Ocean and can be found between Norway and Russia. Among many things, it's home to one of the largest colonies of seabirds, including puffins and razorbills.

Something special starts happening in the Barents Sea during the spring that benefits us all. And it's all thanks to a tiny organism called phytoplankton (FIE-to-plank-ton).

Phytoplankton are like the ocean's plants (their name means "drifting plants" in Greek!). Just like plants on land, they need sunlight and air to grow. Both land plants and phytoplankton use chlorophyll (KLOR-ah-fil) to take in sunlight for photosynthesis (fo-to-SIN-thuh-sis), which is how they create their own food!

Phytoplankton also take in the carbon dioxide in the air to help them grow, and "breathe" out clean oxygen, just like trees. During most of the year, phytoplankton don't get enough sunlight, but in the spring and summer, they "bloom" so much that they can be seen from space! And when they bloom, they pull more carbon dioxide out of the air, cleaning more than 50 percent of the air we breathe.

Talk about a breath of fresh air!

Fun Fact
Millions of phytoplankton can fit in a drop of water—they're that small!

Yoga Time

1 Start on your hands and knees.

2 Step forward with one foot.

3 Lift yourself up and put your hands on your front knee, or raise your arms up to the sky!

4 Breathe in and out three times.

5 Bring your hands back down on the floor.

6 Bring your foot back so you're on your hands and knees again.

7 Repeat on the other side.

You did it!

Mindful Moment

Let's do flower breathing. Pretend your hand is a flower about to bloom.

1 Hold out your hand palm facing up as if you're about to receive a gift.

2 Slowly close your hand until your fingertips touch. Your hand should look like a flower bud now.

3 Let your flower slowly bloom: Open your hand again. This time, breathe with your movement.

4 Breathe in as you close your flower.

5 Breathe out as you open your flower.

6 Keep slowly opening and closing your flower, breathing in and out.

7 Stop whenever you'd like.

How do you feel right now?

You can do flower breathing anytime, all you need is your hand-y flower (see what I did there?).

Mirror, Mirror on the Web...

Have you ever seen a full spiderweb sparkling in the sun? It's one of nature's many amazing wonders. Just as amazing is how many types of spiders exist!

Pretend you're a spider spinning a web as you trace the number path for the Calm Down Countdown. Trace the path with your finger, breathing in with the purple numbers and out with the green numbers.

Breathe in...   10   8   6   4   2

Breathe out...   9   7   5   3   1

Spiders play an important role in our ecosystem. They keep farm crops healthy by feeding on insects that might destroy them. Their webs catch insects that can carry disease, such as flies and mosquitoes. Spider silk and venom have even helped scientists create medicines and treat illnesses.

In Australia, you can find the unique mirror spider. It's tiny, less than a quarter of an inch long.

While some spider venom can be deadly, the mirror spider's venom is not so dangerous to humans. What stands out is how these spiders appear: They have silvery legs that almost look translucent (some light can be seen through them) and their abdomens are colorful and shiny!

Scientists have observed colors like red, yellow, green and cream on this little spider. The shine comes from tiny crystal-like guanine, which comes from their, um, waste. Instead of passing it out through their poop, the guanine comes out right under the abdomen's thin skin, which makes it easy to see. This might sound gross, but the results are beautiful and serve a purpose: The sparkling scales on the mirror spider's body help protect it from predators by distracting and confusing them with the reflecting light.

Yoga Time

1 Stand with your feet very wide apart.

2 Bend your knees and put your hands on the ground between your feet. If your feet are not flat on the floor, move them a little farther apart.

3 Stay here, reach your hands to the opposite sides and rest them on the floor or hold onto opposite legs.

4 Stay here for five to 10 breaths. You can also gently rock from side to side or try balancing on your tippy toes.

5 When you're ready, uncross your arms (if they're crossed) and slowly sit down.

Mindful Moment

Check with your grown-up before doing this activity.

What You Need
Sidewalk chalk or painter's/masking tape

❶ Make an outline of a spiderweb on the sidewalk with chalk or on the carpet with tape. It can be a simple "X" or a more complicated web.

❷ Walk along the web mindfully and slowly, walking heel to toe. Try to pay attention to the feeling of your feet on the ground as you walk. Once you've finished, try doing it backward!

I'm So Excited,
and I Just Can't Hide It!

Trace the path with your finger, breathing in with the purple numbers and out with the green numbers.

Breathe in...   10   8   6   4   2

Breathe out...   9   7   5   3   1

Have you heard of BIG emotions or feelings? These are feelings like anger or anxiety that feel bigger than others and can be more difficult to deal with.

Excitement can be a big emotion, too, even though it's a good feeling. We usually get excited when something fun is about to happen, like our birthday, summer vacation or a party! But excitement can become a much bigger emotion when we get too excited and can't control our reactions (what we say and do).

What happens when you feel excited?

• Your heart beats faster.

• Your emotions can feel stronger and more powerful.

- You become extra alert and feel more energetic.

- You start breathing faster.

Sometimes this can lead us to make quick choices without thinking things through. That's why we need to be mindful and aware of how we're feeling so we can make smart choices.

Yoga Time

1 Stand up.

2 Bring your feet out wide. Point your right toes out to the side.

3 Bring your arms out to the sides.

4 Touch your right fingers to the floor in front of your right foot (or you can gently touch your right ankle or foot—get as close as you can).

5 Reach your left arm straight up.

6 Look up at your left thumb.

7 After taking three breaths in and out, come back up to standing, then try it on the other side.

Mindful Moment

TAKE FIVE!

Mindfulness is good for us in so many ways. One way is to let us press pause on our day so that we give ourselves time to breathe and think. When we feel very excited, it can be hard to slow down during the fun. Try practicing this during moments when you're already feeling calm or any time you think it could help. All you need is your breath!

Before you need to do something, "take five": take five breaths. Try it now!

Sit comfortably. Put one hand on your heart and one hand on your belly, then take five deep breaths, feeling your belly rise and fall with each breath.

Do this before you get up in the morning, before you have to take a test or do something challenging, when you're about to go somewhere or whenever you'd like. Taking that time to breathe will help you feel calmer and ready for whatever you're doing next.

What else helps you calm down?

Interview With Taro Roots
Dasheen and Eddoe

Trace the path with your finger, breathing in with the purple numbers and out with the green numbers.

Breathe in...   10   8   6   4   2

Breathe out...   9   7   5   3   1

Meet two totally tubular taro root friends: Dasheen and Eddoe! Hello!

DASHEEN: Oh, hey there!

EDDOE: Hi!

Can you tell our friend here a bit more about yourselves?

DASHEEN: Of course! I'm one variety of taro root called dasheen. Sometimes people call me "elephant ears" because that's what my leaves look like!

EDDOE: And I'm a taro root, too! What's my nickname?

DASHEEN: You're another variety called eddoe. We're both root vegetables.

EDDOE: Root vegetables?

DASHEEN: That just means that the part that is eaten grows underground.

EDDOE: Oh, like carrots and potatoes?

DASHEEN: Bingo, Eddoe. But the part of a taro root that you eat is not actually a root, it's called a corm. Corms are short, round stems that grow underground and have an important job: to store nutrients for the entire plant!

EDDOE: Ooh, what kind of nutrients?

DASHEEN: Taro roots have a lot of fiber and protein. Even our pretty heart-shaped leaves can be cooked! Some people have also used us for medicine to help them feel better. And you know what, there's even an ancient Hawaiian story that says that taro is actually a child who became a plant and went on to help the first people in Hawaii!

EDDOE: Okay, that's it, I'm calling it: We're definitively superfoods!

You certainly are! Thank you for talking to us, taro roots!

DASHEEN

Did You Know?

Taro is toxic if you eat it without cooking it properly first!

Yoga Time

❶ Crouch down in a ball.

❷ Pretend your feet are rooted to the ground.

❸ Slowly start to grow tall until you're standing up.

❹ Reach your arms up to the sky.

❺ Wiggle your fingers!

❻ Take a breath and smile at the sun (or moon).

❼ Try it again and grow even slower this time.

Mindful Moment

DRAWING TO MUSIC

What You Need
- Music
- Pencil, crayons or markers
- Paper

1 For one minute, put on some music and draw lines, squiggles, shapes, anything that comes to mind.
You don't have to draw any one thing, just move your pencil with the flow of the music.

2 Stop the music and look at your drawing motions!

Try this again with the same song or a different tune!

My Mindful Music Art

Niagara Falls

Let's get ready to learn about waterfalls by taking a few deep breaths...

Trace the path with your finger, breathing in with the purple numbers and out with the yellow numbers.

Breathe in...   10   8   6   4   2

Breathe out...   9   7   5   3   1

Most of these natural wonders are formed as a river flows near a cliff, eroding the rock over time until the water can flow freely over the cliff. Niagara Falls is a famous waterfall located between two countries: Canada and the United States. The Falls are about 12,000 years old, and the water comes from the Great Lakes.

We can think of meditation like being behind a

waterfall of thoughts—the goal is to sit back a
nd enjoy the view without getting pummeled by
the fast-moving water. When we meditate,
we can notice our thoughts flowing past us
without experiencing them all at once, which can
feel overwhelming.

Try closing your eyes and imagine you're sitting
behind a waterfall. Pretend that the water rushing
past you is your thoughts. You have some space from
them and can see and hear them as they come
and go. Just notice them. Any time you
notice a thought come up, observe it and
let it flow away. No need to think about
whether it's a good or bad thought,
just let it go for now.

Come back to your imaginary thought
waterfall whenever you need a break.

Yoga Time

1 Stand up tall.

2 Place your hands on your hips.

3 Get steady on one leg, then slowly raise the other leg out straight in front of you.

4 Hold for three breaths.

5 Bring your leg down. Shake out your arms and legs.

6 Try it on the other side.

Do this as many times as you'd like.

Mindful Moment

BALANCING ACT!

What You Need
- Beanbag or stuffed animal
- Jump rope or masking tape

Mindfulness is not always about sitting still and breathing. You can be mindful while doing everyday things, as long as you're focused on the present moment and treating yourself with kindness rather than judgment.

Some adventurous people have walked on a tightrope over Niagara Falls! That takes a lot of practice and balance.

Here are a couple of balancing acts you can try out yourself:

- Make a line on the floor with your jump rope or masking tape. Walk forward and backward on it, following the line.

- Balance the beanbag or stuffed animal on your head, then try walking forward slowly. Then backward. See if you can walk the whole line without dropping it!

Red Panda

Let's start with the Calm Down Countdown.

Trace the path with your finger, breathing in with the purple numbers and out with the green numbers.

Breathe in... 10   8   6   4   2

Breathe out...   9   7   5   3   1

With their reddish fur, black legs, white ears and face markings, red pandas have a distinct look. Although their name includes the word panda, these mammals are more closely related to raccoons and weasels than the panda bear you might be thinking of. Red pandas live in the Himalayan mountains in Nepal, Myanmar and parts of China.

These animals are endangered, but they don't have many predators because they're hard to find. They live really high up in trees and spend most of their days eating bamboo. Red pandas also enjoy eating fruit, grass, insects, bird eggs and small lizards. Bamboo contains cellulose, which red pandas can't digest (their bodies aren't able to break down the

food to absorb its nutrients).
That means they need to eat a
lot of it in order to have enough
energy for the day. In fact,
red pandas spend most of their
day finding and eating food. Can
you imagine spending a day scarfing
down meal after meal like that?

One more thing about red pandas—they're acrobats!
They have a special wrist bone that acts like a
thumb so they can hold onto tree branches better.
Red pandas also rely on their tails to keep
their balance.

Are you ready for a balancing challenge?
Turn to the next page to grow tall like bamboo!

Fun Fact

Various trees in China, Nepal, India and Myanmar are covered in a red lichen, so the red pandas' fur helps them camouflage and blend right in!

Yoga Time

1 Stand up tall.

2 Start to balance on one leg, then bring your other foot to a) your ankle, b) the side of your leg or c) the inside of your thigh (just not on your knee).

3 Place your hands on your waist or press your palms together in front of your heart.

4 Focus on keeping your balance. If you want, slowly raise your hands up to the sky, growing tall like a tree...or bamboo!

5 Gently put your foot down. Try this again, but this time, balance on the other leg. How tall can you grow while standing still?

Mindful Moment

Red pandas spend a lot of time on their own. What do you imagine they think about (besides eating!)?

It's important to take the time to pause every day and check in with ourselves, asking: How am I feeling? Why? Can I put a name to it—like excited, upset, lonely, hopeful or creative—or is it many feelings at the same time? Is whatever I'm doing right now what I want or need to be doing at this moment? What do I want to happen next? How can I make that happen?

Each day, fill in a block of the Mindful Month Map to see how your emotions change over time. Pick the color that represents your strongest emotion for that day. If your emotion isn't listed, label an unassigned block and use that color.

SUNDAY	MONDAY	TUESDAY	WEDNESDAY	THURSDAY	FRIDAY	SATURDAY

Excited   Happy   Neutral   Angry   Sad

Loving   Annoyed   _____   _____   _____

4 Mindful Activities You Can Try Anytime

WHAT DO YOU SEE?

Make your own telescope to help you focus on one thing at a time.

What You Need
• Paper towel roll or paper and tape, markers or crayons (optional)

1 Decorate the paper towel roll or paper with any design you'd like: stripes, polka dots or anything that will show up well once the paper is rolled up.

2 If you are using paper, roll the paper into a cylinder. Put tape along the sides so it keeps its shape.

3 Look through your new telescope. What do you see? Find something to focus on and just look at it for 10 seconds. What do you notice about it? Pay attention to the colors, the shape, the texture. When you're done, try it with a different object in the room!

SINGING TREE

Have you heard about the Singing Tree? It's any tree in your neighborhood that birds hang out in. You might not be able to see them at first, but you can hear their beautiful song!

What You Need
- A tree

1 Take a walk with your grown-up. Pay attention to the sounds you hear along the way.

2 Look for a tree where birds are singing. When you find one, slowly walk closer so they don't fly away.

3 In a safe place, close your eyes if you'd like and listen to the birdsong. What does it sound like? Does the song have a pattern? Do you hear more than one bird? Do you hear different types of songs? How many birds do you think are in the tree?

The great thing about finding singing trees is that you might start recognizing songs and noticing the same birds coming back. Hello, bird buddies!

MAGIC WAND BREATHING

Abracadabra! Add a little mindful magic to your breathing.

What You Need
• A pencil or stick, yarn or ribbon, glue

1 Decorate your pencil or stick by gluing yarn or ribbons to the end (add other craft supplies if you'd like).

2 When your magic wand is ready, test it out:

When the wand moves up, breathe in.

When the wand moves down, breathe out.

When the wand moves from side to side, hold your breath.

3 Try these patterns. Can you follow along with your wand...and your breath?

Bring out your magic wand whenever you want to practice magic breathing. Try it with someone else and take turns moving the wand!

YOU CAN RING MY BELL

Play this mindfulness game when you want to relax!

What You Need
• A bell or singing bowl, or you can ask a grown-up to help you find "mindfulness bell" sounds on YouTube

1 Sit in a comfortable position. Have someone play the bell sound and close your eyes.

2 Pay attention to the bell sound, and when you can't hear it anymore, put up your hand.

3 Try it again! You'll find that you'll be able to hear the bell sound longer and longer each time.

4 Switch places so you can challenge someone else to listen to the bell sound!

Acknowledgments

The team at Media Lab Books is wonderfully supportive and talented. Thank you to Jules, Jeff, Miki, Courtney, Susan and, of course, Phil, who was the first to believe that this little podcast could become a book. Thank you also to Cory Reid for providing such beautiful illustrations. I'm so grateful.

Finally, I want to thank Rob Griffiths of *Bedtime FM* for introducing me to the wonderful world of kids' podcasting and helping create *Peace Out* at the start.

About the Author

CHANEL TSANG is an educator and family supports practitioner. She has worked with children and families in school and community programs for more than 20 years and currently works in a research center focused on child development and mental health at the University of Toronto.

A lifelong learner and certified yoga teacher, Chanel is currently pursuing a master's degree in adult education and community development.

CHECK OUT THE PODCAST

Scan the QR code to start listening to *Peace Out Podcast* episodes!

About the Illustrator

CORY REID has a BA (Hons) in illustration from Loughborough University, UK, and creates adorable characters and worlds for them to inhabit in his charming textured style. Cory has illustrated titles for clients including Usborne Publishing, Owlet Press, Autumn Publishing and Pan Macmillan.

Media Lab Books
For inquiries, call 646-449-8614

Published by Topix Media Lab
14 Wall Street, Suite 3C
New York, NY 10005

Printed in China

ISBN-13: 978-1-956403-28-2
ISBN-10: 1-956403-28-0